# The Colors Of Our Family Quilt

# The Colors Of Our Family Quilt

Velma Akins

**To order additional copies of this book, contact:**
Xlibris Corporation
1-888-795-4274
www.Xlibris.com
Orders@Xlibris.com
69894

# CONTENTS

# CHAPTER 1

## It Don't Matter Anyway

The year 2008 was a year of changes. Our Country elected it first black President, President Obama. My youngest son Elijah started High School and my oldest son Josiah was moving out on his own.

It was a cold December day, a week before Christmas as I recall. The air outside seemed to be as crisp and sharp as a razor. The time of year that always made me wish I could hibernate until spring. Everyone always seems to be in a rush around Christmas, our household even more this year than ever.

Josiah would be moving to Texas after the New Year. He was going to get his Masters Degree like his dad. He would be attending SMU in January.

My husband Roland, a Pastor of a little storefront church here in Kansas, was the first one that I know of in our family to get a Masters Degree and my sons seemed to want to excel academically as he did. My husband and I had moved from Pennsylvania to Kansas about twenty years ago. God has been our Rock through good times and bad. We pray that He will be that Rock for our sons also.

As Josiah packed his belongings to move them to Texas, he ask if he could have some family photos to take with him. I remembered I had made two copies of an old photo of my father, one for each of my sons. I knew he was only asking for one of me, his dad, and his brother, but you know how that is. I looked high and low for those copies. I looked through album after album. As I looked, memory after memory came flowing back to my mind. I found four generations of photos from my husband's side of the family and my side. It seem to me as a wonderful, colorful tapestry of people, like a quilt that made up the fabric of our family. I can truly hear the Lord say to me "Thelma, life is just a hands breath". I knew those generations would be lost, like old pieces torn from our family quilt.

My boys looked at the old photo sitting on the fireplace of my father and a friend of his and they ask "who are those people in the zootsuits?". My father died when I was just thirteen years old but his memory is still very vivid in my mind. I told them it was a photo of my father and his best friend. I asked them to guess who in the photo was their grandfather. They didn't know and Eli said "I guess it don't matter anyway". It mattered to me, but I found myself saying the same thing when I came across a photo that my mother had sent me about two years ago of my grandmother and her sister. My grandmother had died before I was born. My grandmother and aunt were young women in their twenties or thirties on the photo. I didn't know who was who. I thought to myself, it really don't matter but then I remember my son's words and I made it matter. I called my seventy five year old mom and asked her. She remembered the photo and much, much more, she had family stories that went back to the days of slavery. Stories that I knew would soon be lost to our family, just as quilting, making sweet grass baskets, knitting, and baking banana nut bread have gone. I can't bake banana nut bread like my mom, I can't quilt like my grandmother, make sweet grass baskets or fan rice like my India, Geechee and African ancestors. I'm not a writer, but I can add a stitch or two to the stories of our colorful family quilt.

# CHAPTER 2

## Going North

My great grandmother, Selma and her sisters Millie and Mariana was born in Montgomery Alabama. Mariana was the older of the three sisters. I don't know how many sisters and brothers they had. I know it had to be at least four of them because they had a brother who died when he was a little child. Aunt Mariana, who looked to be more Indian than black, was married to a man named Emanuel.

Aunt Millie, as we called her, quickly became like the matriarch of our family. She raised Grandma Rose as her own child when she was born.

Grandma Rose was Mama Selma's first child. My grandma Rose was tall, very light skin with little freckles on her face. She looked very much like Mama Selma's mother who looked to be Creole or Indian and black mixed. Rose had two brother. The oldest brother was raised by his father, the youngest one was raised by Mama Selma. I Don't think Mama Selma was much on raising kids but she did what she had to do. Mama Selma took the youngest son up North to Pennsylvania to raise him.

Aunt Millie was a short, dark skin woman. She was soft-spoken in her ways. Grandma Rose on the other hand, seemed to be proud, with a obsession about cleaning (she cleaned all the time) and just a dash of vanity. Aunt Millie became a mother and father to Rose.

Rose began seeing Willis, a tall, dark, nice looking man. Willis and Rose's relationship didn't last, but they did have a son together, my father. When he was born he looked just like his father. Rose named him Jacob Lee Williamson. If Willis married another woman or not, I don't know. Willis was not spoken of much after that. Rose married more than a couple of times without the benefit of divorcing between marriages.

Grandma Rose, Jacob Lee, and Aunt Millie went north to live with
Mama Selma. She wanted Rose to help her with a boarding house she had.
Rose was a very good cook and hard worker. Although Mama Selma only
wanted Rose to come north, Rose said she would never leave her child and
mother (Aunt Millie) behind.

Grandma's youngest brother moved to New York. When Mama Selma
died, Grandma sent word to her brother in New York about the passing of
their Mother. Rose received a letter of sympathy from her brother saying
more or less "Sorry to hear about the passing of your Mother. You have my
sympathy". He never returned for the funeral.

Jacob Lee remained an only child of my Grandma Rose. They spoiled
him as much as any child could ever be spoiled. I can recall a story once
told to me about my dad. It was Christmas Eve, and he was about three
or four years old. Aunt Millie and Grandma Rose just could not get him
to go to bed. He wanted to play in his snow boots. I think they spared the
rod a little too much. They told him over and over that Santa was coming
and he would not get toys if Santa saw him running around like that. A
knock came at the door and Jacob Lee ran as fast as he could to his bed. He
couldn't get his boots off so he jumped in to the bed, boots and all. They
had no more problems with him that night.

# CHAPTER 3

## Jacob's Branch

Jacob was once a boxer, a preacher, a steel mill worker, sold beer out of his house, a shay tree mechanic, a self-appointed "professor" and even in the military at one time. Jacob put his age up from about fourteen years old to eighteen to get into the military because he was to young to go. When he was in the military he looked up his father, Wilson. I don't think that meeting went well. He did say he had other siblings younger than he was and he got a photo of his father but he didn't want to talk much about him. He started drinking during his time in the military.

My dad married his first wife Esther, a nice looking dark skin woman during his time as a boxer. They had two kids, Jacob jr. and Kathy. My dad and Esther liked to drink and party too much. Alcohol was not my dad's friend, he became abusive to Esther. Alcohol effected ever part of his life. He didn't make it big as a boxer and their marriage didn't make it either. Grandma and Aunt Millie raised Jacob jr. and Kathy.

Jacob worked for US Steel and as a shay tree mechanic on the side when he had the time. Generations after generations of people worked for US Steel before it was outsourced. The Steel Mill was a place were molten hot steel, glowing orange from the intense heat of the furnaces, ran through troughs to make ingots. The air seemed to be always filled with a fine silver colored dust. The glittering dust covered everything, and the language spoken in that place would make a refined man blush (not that my dad was a refined man).

My mom was Jacob Lee's second wife, Beth. Jacob jr., who was about eleven at the time and Kathy, who was about twelve, were very happy to have a new Mom in the house. Beth was a light caramel color with dusty brown, long hair and a face that looked younger than her years. She was small in frame but strong, not frail at all. She was not a big eater, my mom ate from a saucer, that is until grandma Rose and Aunt Millie happened to her life. They would say "Betty Ann, (I don't know were they got that name from) ya don eat enough ta keep a bod alive". That and six kids were the end of that small frame. Beth and Jacob had four girls, Victoria, Maria, Thelma and Adeline, also David, a son who died as a new born. My youngest sister Alexis Mare was born six years after Adeline.

Jacob jr. got a job as a paperboy just as many boys do. He had to get up before the sun, about four thirty or five o'clock in the morning. He had to go get his papers, bundle them in rubber bands and then deliver them before six in the morning. Getting up that early was to much for Brother, the name we called Jacob Jr. One day there came knocking at the door. My Mom, Beth answered and there stood Brother's boss "Mrs. Williamson, I'm so sorry to hear about your loss" he said with a sorrowful look on his face. "What loss?" my mother replied, thinking this man had to be confused. "why, the loss of your son" he responded, thinking maybe the grief was getting to her. "What son?" said my mother, knowing this man was confused. The man, beginning to feel somewhat confused, said "Jacob told me that his little brother had passed away and that is why he couldn't come to work". My mother informed the man that Jacob jr. never had a baby brother. She went on to say "he is the baby brother". Well, needless to say, that was the end of Brother's paperboy job.

The only grandfather I can remember is Bob Browning, we called him Daddy Bob. When grandma Rose and Daddy Bob were getting ready to marry, grandma sent my dad to pick up her blood test from the Dr's office. Jacob Lee asked the receptionist if she had the test results for Rose Sharp. She answered "no". He asked for every last name he could think of her having, but the answer came back no. The receptionist said we do have a Rose Green's test results. Embarrassed, he said "that's her, give me that one". He later told my mother "I don't even know where she got my last name (Williamson) from". Aunt Millie didn't know were the name came from either. I guess my grandma's philosophy was "what's in a name, a rose by any other still smells as sweet". Grandma had a last name everyone could remember after she married Daddy Bob, she became Rose Lee Browning.

Daddy Bob was born in the South. He looked all together like a white man although he was half black. He was the poor unfortunate product of a rape. He was raised by his mother and her husband, a black man.

Every time his biological father, who was the town sheriff, saw Bob he was reminded of his wrong that he had done, so he ran Bob out of town.

Aunt Millie didn't care much for Daddy Bob because of how he looked. She did all she knew how to do to run him off. She would call him names like old white hunky and things like that. Mostly he took the frail old lady's verbal abuse without saying a word. The older ones of my family seem to have a language of their own. One day Aunt Millie started in on him "I don know weh Rose gat ya from, ya ol white hunky". Daddy Bob could take no more, so he said in a slow southern draw "alright black gal". Aunt Millie's blood began to boil. She grabbed a soda pop bottle from a nearby table and raise it to hit Daddy Bob in the head with it. My mom, who was in the living room with them at the time, grabbed Aunt Millie's arm to stop her. My mother asked my father, who was also in the living room, "didn't he see Aunt Millie ready to hit Daddy Bob?". He replied "That wasn't my business". My mom said "and if he would have hit her back?". Dad responded "that would be my business". Bob loved Rose too much to be run off by Aunt Millie and Dad.

My sister Victoria was born in May of 1958 after our parents were married about seven years. She was a light brown baby with coal black, loosely curled hair. Vickie talked before she could even walk. "Aht, aht Cookie, don touch dat Cookie" she would say as she was about to touch something she shouldn't have. Cookie was Vic's nickname as a child. Daddy Bob thought she was better than sliced bread. He would say "Dat baby is smarter dan a grownup". She talked early and talked a lot, truth be told, she still does.

By the time Vic was born, Kathy had married and had her first son Roland that same year. Although her and brother always called Beth mom and Esther by her first name, Kathy began to take up more time with Esther than she had in the past.

Maria was born to my parents in September of 1959. She was a nice round, short, little brown baby. Maria always had her thumb in her mouth. From the time she could get out of her bed by herself, she would get up and wait by the front door for my dad to come home from work ( no matter what shift he happened to be working). With a smile that could make any hard work day brighter, she would look up at him. He would look at Maria and say "Hay, sister full bosom". Maria couldn't tell time, but her heart always knew when her dad was coming home.

My Parents became members of Zion Holiness Church around the time we were coming along. My dad even began preaching every now and then. It wasn't easy for daddy to leave his old drinking buddies alone. They would tell him "ah man, you jus hen pecked. You can come to the bar with us and set and talk. Ya don have ta drink". Setting and talking didn't work, in time he was drinking also.

I was born in August of 1960. I had wavy black hair, brown skin and big dark brown eyes that watered a lot. My mom said I looked as ugly as a frog peeping through ice. Soon my wavy hair turned into big curls that looked as if I had just came from the hair dresser's shop. I never wanted anyone to touch my hair, truth be told, I still don't like my hair done much now.

Adeline was born in July of 1961. She was light brown, with dark brown hair and two fingers in her mouth at all times. She was bold in every thing she did.

Norris was born a little time after I was in 1960 to my sister Kathy. She and her husband were no longer together when Norris came along. Kathy was staying with her mother Esther.

David was born to Mom and Dad two months early in 1962. He died before they could take him home.

Kathy became ill and died around the same time David died and they were buried together. Kathy's sons were raised separately. Roland was raised by his father's parents and Norris was raised by Esther.

I can remember my father, Jacob crying a lot over Kathy's death when he had been drinking. I didn't remember Kathy, but it would make me sad just to hear him cry like that.

Jacob also had a bit of a devious side to him. He would say to me and my sister in a sad voice "I'm going to Hawaii". Not knowing what or where Hawaii was, we would plead with him "Don't go to Hawaii daddy. Please don't go !". He would respond "Gat ta go". We would begin crying, as we thought Hawaii had to be an awful place to keep a person's father there and never let him come back. Knowing what I know now, it was just a game he was playing with us. I wish I could go to Hawaii. "Gat ta go".

One day there came a nock at the door. My mother answered it and there stood two little old white ladies. They asked my mother if the "Professor" was in. My mom said "Who? The Professor? There's no Professor living here". Grandma Rose said "Day lookin fo Tee tee", a nickname she always called my dad. Grandma told the ladies that he would be home later. I don't know who in the right mind would pay that "Professor" for advice, but I guess like the saying "there's a sucker born every minute".

# CHAPTER 4

## Grandma's House

My parents separated when I was three years old. We would always visit grandma Rose and daddy every weekend. I can hear grandma now "sit back baby". Our feet barely hung over the end of the sofa. "don put ya feet on de do foe baby" she would say. "Do foe" is what she called the sofa. Toys were always called play pretties for some reason. My grandma could see a string on the floor a mile away and out would come the hand sweeper. Daddy Bob would talk a lot about the "O stock and de new stock" to people and write something down on paper. Later I found out that the "O stock and new stock" was the old stock and the new stock and Daddy Bob was a numbers man (sold numbers). Daddy Bob would take us to the Five and Ten store to get coloring books and to eat, all the time talking to people about the "o stock and de new stock".

I can remember my mom telling us that grandma Rose had sugar. We didn't understand what that was exactly, so we asked her "did Daddy Bob have salt". Grandma Rose always had candy gummy orange slices on her dresser. One day we asked her could we have some of her candy. She replied, "Oh ya won't like dat candy baby". I thought what kid won't like candy. After we persisted, she gave in and gave us some of the candy. We popped the candy in our months and to our horror the candy was covered in salt not sugar. What kind of sick mind would come up with such a device of cruelty to ones tastes buds. Needless to say, we never asked her for more.

Thinking back, I guess it was hard to keep four little girl entertained and out of mischief. My sister Vickie was one of the best when it came to getting into mischief. Vickie said "Daddy Bob, can I do you hair?", they had to cut the comb from his head when she finished trying to make him curls. Vickie said "let's drink grandma's perfume", over forty years later I can still remember that awful taste.

Grandma took out two pieces of cloth, one long and one short, for us to play with. Vickie said "let's have a fashion show and I get the long piece of cloth because I'm bigger". Grandma gave us some safety pins and we went into the bathroom to make our dresses. Vickie wrapped her cloth around and over her shoulder like a Greek goddess or something. My cloth was to short for all that and I didn't want to have the same dress as my sister anyway. I put the cloth around me, pulling the cloth together front to back at the shoulders and my sister pinned it, leaving a loop for my arms to go through on each side. I pinned it closed down the front of me. It looked like a dress but not one that a goddess would ever let herself be found dead in. Vic said "I'll go out first and then you come out". I could hear the family as they ooohed and awed over Vic's dress. I looked in the mirror, that was on the back of the bathroom door, at myself and thought I looked like a homeless child. My sister's voice called "Thelma, its your turn". I came out expecting the worse but then my grandmother said "Oh Thelma, dat dress looks as good as some dresses ya see on folks today" then she called me her fashion plate. My smile couldn't get any bigger if I tried, even though I didn't know what a fashion plate was.

My father Jacob started dating a lady name Tammy. He moved in with her and sold beer from her house. He could no longer work in the steel mill because he had TB. When he was drunk he would tell Tammy that he would always love Beth. He stayed drunk most of the time. I can remember me and my sisters visiting my dad, most of our visits he was drunk and beating up on Tammy for little or no good reason. This one particular visit stands out in my mind because of the ridiculousness of their behavior. My father was at the kitchen table drinking. Tammy came over to him and placed her hand on the top of his balding head and slapped it with her other hand. Jacob jumped up and began hitting her. He told Tammy to sit down on a stool in the living room. Then he proceeded to gently manipulate her head into a upright position, instructing her to hold her head just like that. As Tammy held her head in the position he had instructed her to do, he slapped her face. Again Jacob repeated his actions two or three time as Tammy held her head just as she had been instructed. I couldn't help but wonder why they were together, but they weren't for much longer after that.

One year, in December of 1967, we got a real baby for Christmas. That year my younger sister Adeline and I had to go to grandma's house for Christmas. Vickie and Maria went to Dad's house. I was thinking how would Santa know were we were this year for Christmas but I knew he would at lest leave us something with mom at our house. Mom had to go get the new baby, but I knew she would be back home by the time Santa came. When we all got to grandma's house she got a call telling us that mom had a little girl baby. Mom named her Alexis Mare. We were wanting a boy but we all were happy about the girl. On Christmas morning grandma called "come see what Santa left ya". I thought "Santa? He knew we were here?". Adeline and I went into the living room and on a chair was a basketball and a doll. The doll was beautiful, with a red dress and a hat with a propeller on top of it. If a person could dream hard enough, that doll could fly anywhere, just like a super hero. Adeline picked up the ball and looked at it, like it was the best thing in the world and I picked up the doll. Grandma said "the ball is yours and the doll is Adeline's" and gave her the doll and me the ball. Adeline said "can I play with your ball?". I gave her my ball and she never looked back at the doll. The doll and I went flying off over mountains and cities, stopping just long enough to tell the imaginary citizens about the magic hat on the doll's head and take them for a short ride. Grandma voice interrupted "yall can trade toys if ya'd like, Santa won't mind". You know we said yes to that idea right away.

When we got home there was our new little sister, tiny light brown baby, prettier than any doll. We took the dresses of all our larger dolls and gave them to our new baby as a gift. Alexis was born to be a gymnast. She did so many flips over the side of her crib that my mother had to give it away to keep her from hurting herself. She was always running, jumping and doing flips. She could whistle before she could talk or walk.

Growing up in the sixties was sometimes confusing for a small child. It was a time when Dr. Martin Luther King jr. marched for the right just for us to be treated as human as anyone else. Angry men spouted venomous words of hatred and racism over the TV. The country had its first Catholic President, John F. Kennedy. Men with their hearts poisoned with the history of Jim Crow killed them both, but the wind of change had already began to blow.

Aunt Millie had two or three strokes before she pasted away from one of them in April of 1971. I can't remember going to her funeral, but I do recall how sick she was before she pasted. She had become as helpless as a new born baby. It was sad to see her like that. Her eyes saw her people move from the back of the bus to the front, and she saw her people learned to read and write beside all other children.

My grandmother Rose died of a sugar coma some time in about 1972. I don't think we kids went to her funeral. It was like she was just gone, never to be seen again. My grandfather seemed to cry a lot after grandma's death and say "I wish I would da died with Rose" or he would say "Rose why you have to die and leave me". It always made me sad to hear him say that. It was almost like he thought she died just to leave him.

My father died in 1974, two years after grandma Rose died. My father had been renting a room from a miss Doty. Miss Doty was a nice older lady who seem to be a good friend to my father. I don't recall him ever drinking alcohol at miss Doty's house or ever fighting with her. He had became very ill from the TB and needed to use oxygen everyday. It was most hard on my sister Vickie because she was his favorite. Sometimes I felt like a child that just happen to be born and I think it effected the way I grieved. As my father became weaker, every movement seemed to be painful for him and Vickie would cry to see him like that. I didn't cry, not even at his funeral. I did love him, he was my dad.

Before he died he gave Vickie his Bible that he had used when he would preach. I don't think he knew that she would someday become a Preacher or maybe he did. When Vickie was three or four, she and my sister Maria would fight over who should be the Preacher when we would play church. I was always the congregation because I was too little to know what was going on. Now, Vickie is a pastor of a church in the Pittsburgh area and Maria preaches from time to time in the church that she attends.

# CHAPTER 5

## The Dent Family

When my mom and dad separated, my mom moved us to the housing projects. There were two housing projects in the small town where we lived. The larger one was very near the elementary school and was more diverse than the smaller housing project where we lived. The smaller one seem to set down in a valley with clay hills circling on three sides of the projects. Two long building ran down either side of a playground, a parking lot, and one road that lead in and out of the projects.

Two of my mother's sisters also lived in the same housing projects that we lived in. Aunt Frannie had seven kids, all of them older than us and aunt Adeline had seven kids, five older and two younger. My mother also had another sister, aunt Flora and three younger brothers, uncle Robson, uncle Edwin, and uncle Geordie. Aunt Flora and uncle Alfred had one kid, a girl the same age as my sister Vickie. Uncle Robson and aunt Lilia had three kids, uncle Edwin had about six kids (two grew up in the same projects we did), and uncle Geordie had five kids.

My mother's family name was Dent. We came from Georgia rice growers. My family are descendents of slaves from the Bi Aka and Bekola African tribes. They are said to be the oldest haplo group in the world and the greatest elephant hunters on the Ivory Cost. They were good at finding medicines to help the sick, but all this didn't keep my ancestors from their destiny with slave ships.

Noldy and Jennie Dent, my great, great grandparents, were born near the end of slavery in Georgia. They had seven kids, my great grandfather Saul was the oldest. Slavery had ended by the time my great grandfather was born. I'm told that the Dent Plantation still stands in Georgia today.

My great grandfather Saul Dent fell in love with Cassie Walker and they were married. She was half Sioux blackfoot and half African American. They had nine kids together, four boys and five girls. She would tell her family stories about her parents. Her father didn't want to work all his life on someone's land as a sharecropper and not have anything that he and his family could call their own. His parents and many generations before them worked their fingers to the bone on the land of their slave masters with only heartache and maybe a back striped from the overseer's whip to show for it. Sharecroppers worked the same land that their parents who were slaves did and lived most of the time in the same cabins that once housed slave families. Great, great grandfather Charles Walker was determined to do better for his family in his generation. He would cut buttons off old clothes, put them in matching sets and sold them. As he worked hard to making his money, he could see a vision of a better life. He was able to buy his own farm with the money he made from selling the buttons. Great, great grandma Jennie Walker's family had not suffered the pains of slavery as they were Sioux. The Sioux lived in bands or groups on land that stretched from Alberta Canada to the Dakotas of the United States. If they were unhappy with their group that they lived with, they were free to move on. The Native American Indian knew very well what it was like to suffer and fight just for the right to exist and to have land of their own to live on. I don't know how Charles and Jennie met, but I do know the Walkers found strength in one another. Although they didn't always agree with each other, they loved each other. When great grandmother Cassie's mother and father would have a falling out with one another, her mother would go outside and put up her tipi to live in until she was no longer angry, then she would go back to her husband. One thing about it, if she was in her tipi or in her house, it was her land and no one would make her move to a reservation.

There was a time when it was against the law for an African American and Native American Indian to marry, but if they chose to do so they would have to endure racism and excommunicated from the Native American Indian group that they were a part of.

Saul jr., Saul and Cassie's oldest son worked on great, great grandfather Walker's farm as a sharecropper. Eventually Saul jr. and his wife Allie inherited it when they passed away.

When Saul and Cassie Dent separated, most of their children were grown. Saul and two of their four son's, Edwin and Wilson, moved to Youngstown, Ohio. My grandfather Robson and his five sister, Lynda,

Frannie, Julina, Ruthie Beth, and Jennie moved to Pittsburgh Pennsylvania with great grandma Cassie. My grandfather Robson said he stayed with his mom to help her and be the man of the house. Robson got a job with US Steel. The Steel mills and the coal mines was where most people worked in Pennsylvania.

A lot of the houses in that day were built without indoor plumbing, a furnace, or electricity. They used oil lamps for light, a fireplace for heat, a wood or coal burning stove to cook on, and a outhouse in the back yard. It's funny, but growing up, I never could understand how so many people around Pittsburgh and Youngstown seemed to be part of our family. It wasn't until I saw a booklet on the Dent family history and talking with my mother was I able to understand a little more about who these people are and how we are even connected to people in Georgia.

My grandfather Robson married the beautiful Victoria "Willa" Hudson, but that's a little ahead of the story. Grandma Willa and her siblings, Geordie, Jameson and Josia came north with their father, Jack Hudson, from the Albany Georgia area. Their sister Sarah Emily came north later. Sarah was a baby and too small for her father to take care of at the time he came north. Jack had been married to Cassie Winfield down in Georgia. They were married at a very young age, Cassie had to be no more that fourteen at the time. Cassie Winfield was one quarter Native American Indian and African American with more than a dash of wild and crazy on the side, with a spirit guide as the cherry on top. She was a young mother as many were back in that day and she wasn't settled in her ways yet. She gave "reading" and sold alcohol, and loved to fight. Great grandfather Jack loved a good fight also but he said he would have to move north or kill great grandma Cassie Winfield, because she would fight him like she was a man.

Jack Hudson was a mystery, he had shinny, black hair with just a little wave to it and caramel brown skin and he spoke with an accent. Sarah would say to our family much later that she thought her father could have been from the West Indies. He was clearly part black anyway and however much black a person had in them, they were black. They say he had been a cowboy at one time and he made home remedies, from spring tonic to thin the blood, to worm candy to keep one from getting worms. Granny from the old TV show about the California Hillbillies had nothing on him when it came to remedies and poultices. They were survivors if nothing more, learning to eat from what they could find around them. They picked Dandelions, Poke Salad, and Elephant ears, they all made good greens.

Rhubarb grew wild and made a nice pie along with apples, cherries, plums and berries that also grew wild. They made gardens on any little patch of dirt they could find. They also kept chickens and hogs if they could.

Grandma Willa and her siblings were chips off the old block when it came to surviving and fighting. I don't think the fighting mattered to much with the Dents because Robson Dent's sister Jennie Dent married Willa's father Jack Hudson and helped him finish raising his kids. Jennie always called Jack Hudson, Mr. Hudson. I guess she called him that because he was so much older than her. She would say she rather be a old man's sweetie than a young man's fool. When Jack went and got Sarah, his youngest, from her grandmother Winfield's house to bring her to live up north, she was so excited. She would finally get to live with her Papa. She would see her sister Willa and her brothers again. Although the trip was long for a little kid, just thinking about her sister and her brothers help to make it seem a little shorter. Everyone was happy to see Sarah, all that is except Josia. Well, after all, this new kid was taking his place as the baby of the family. Sarah would hear her new mother say, when Jack was nowhere around to hear it, "I didn't know Mr. Hudson had another kid, Josia you will always be my baby". It made her sad to hear that, but all in all she was happy to be with her siblings again.

Sometimes a blessing may turn out not to be a blessing after all. Everyone was so excited, Papa had found a bigger house for the family to live in. When I say found a house, they would literally find abandoned houses and move in. Anyway, Geordie was now fourteen and Jameson was thirteen. Although Josia was no more than about nine or ten, it was time the boys had a room separately from the girls. Mama Jennie would get her garden planted right away, because canning time would come before you knew it. Papa would have to go to the nearby woods to gather the plants he needed for medicines. With five kids, Papa would need something to help keep colds and the flu away. He would need something to breakup fevers and congestion just in case they got sick over the winter months.

Not long after settling in to their new house, Geordie became sick with a cough and fever. Papa tried every remedy he could think of and a lot of praying, yet Geordie only seemed to get sicker. Jameson also became ill and Papa was beside himself with worry. He went over and over in his mind the remedies that was passed down to him from generations to generation but nothing seem to help. To the family's heartbreak Geordie died and then Jameson shortly after him. Before the family could dry their tears Sarah became sick. It had to be the house, Mama and Papa thought, and it would not take another child. They moved right away but Sarah remand sickly throughout her youth. Although they found out later that Sarah had Tuberculosis and Diabetes, there was also a global influenza epidemic called "The Great Pandemic" where forty million people worldwide died from it.

One day Mama was cooking beans, cornbread and rice. Beans and rice was one of the meals that was cooked often in a poor man's house. After the food was ready, Mama called the family to the table. Papa and the kids sat down at the table. Josia, who was very spoiled, looked at the beans and turned up his nose. He said "beans again, I don't want beans". Before he could get his words out good, Papa jumped up and punched Josia in the face hard enough to knock him out. Papa replied "what every my lovely wife worked hard to cook, you eat". It may as well have been a gourmet meal because not another complaint arose that day at the table.

Willa grew into a teen with a head full of dreams of young men, as all girls do. Her eyes were set on Robson Dent. He was the bee's knees. Although he was much older than her, he had his eye on her also. She was the cat's meow. They both knew that Papa would never approve of them seeing each other. Robson knew very well of Papa quick temper, but his hormones won out over his head. When Willa became pregnant Papa was furious. He demanded to know who the baby's father was. Willa told him that Robson was the father. With fire in his eyes he went to confront Robson. Robson would have to take care of his responsibilities or answer to Papa's wrath. It was thought to be a shame in those days to have a baby and not be married. When Robson saw Papa, with fury in his face and eyes flashing with anger, Robson's heart leaped out of his chest and into his throat. Papa wanted to know if Robson was the father of Willa's child. Knowing the wrong answer may cause him death or at lest great pain, he denied the baby. Robson's mother Cassie, also with pleading eyes, assured that her son was not the father. What could Papa do but just take care of his family.

Willa had a baby girl in 1925 and named her Flora Jackie Will Dent. Flora was the apple of Papa's eye and the little princess of the Hudson household. No one could chastise Flora as long as Papa was around, not even Willa.

Robson married Willa after the baby was born, she was eighteen and he was twenty seven at the time. He never admitted Flora was his child, that is not when they were around certain family members. Flora continued to live with Papa and Mama until the age of six years old.

# CHAPTER 6

## Robson and Willa, Willa and Robson

The roaring twenties was a time of bootleg liquor and speakeasies. Jazz musicians like Duke Ellington and Al Jolson was some of the most popular music of the day. The dance most popular was the Charleston. Women dressed in flapper style dresses and short hair with a wave in it. In the early twenties indoor plumbing was mostly in upscale homes and fancy hotels. Robson and Willa didn't live in a upscale home, far from it.

It wasn't long before Robson and Willa had another baby girl in 1927, they named her Frannie. Frannie was a pretty, short brown baby, just a little lady. She was never a big talker but always seemed very wise to me. Willa's sister Sarah had a baby girl around the time Willa had Frannie in 1927, but Sarah's baby didn't survive.

Just thinking about what a day in the life of my grandmother must have been like makes me feel tired. She would have to get up more than likely before the sun, wash and feed the baby. She would gather the eggs and cook breakfast on a coal burning stove. Next clean up the kitchen, feed the chickens, and wash at the very less, diapers and baby cloths in a washtub and hang them out to dry. With baby in tow, get some buckets and a little wagon and head for the train yard to glean coal that fell from the trains and onto the tracks. A person could buy coal from the coal wagon when it came around but that took money. She would also have to take time out of her day to go to the waterworks to get water. The waterworks was next to the ice house where people could get ice for their icebox. Don't forget when she made breakfast, lunch, or dinner, it was all from scratch.

Not too long after Frannie was born, then came Adeline in 1928, a little light brown baby, Miss fireball herself. She never was afraid to say what was on her mind and she did every chance she got.

Robson's work in the Steel Mill was steady but very hard backbreaking labor. The shovel became a large part of the laborer's day. Shoveling hot slag out the runners and lining them for the next heat. By the time their shift ended they were covered head to toe with black soot with silver colored specks in it and dog tired.

Papa, Mama and Flora visited them often, bringing homemade goodies and medicines. All of Willa's siblings were on their own by this time but Willa always stayed close with them. She and Sarah were like two peas in a pod.

They both were very good at making clothing, so they always had the latest fashion of their day. In 1930 Willa and Sarah were both expecting, although Sarah's second baby didn't survive either. She didn't have anymore kids until much later. Willa's fourth baby was born in March 1930 and she named her Beth. Robson Dent and Willa broke up before Beth could be born and like Flora, Robson denied Beth also but they were Dent children. Robson moved into his sister's boarding house were his mother also lived but he would visit Willa and the kids when he felt like it. He would tell the kids "Ya'll my boys, dat's why ya gat my name." It would be about four year before Willa would have more kids.

When Flora was about six years old she came to live with Willa and her sisters, Frannie, Adeline, and Beth. Beth was about one, she always looked up to her older sisters. Flora was full of mischief for the lack of a better word. One day, when Beth was about three years old, they were playing in the yard with the chickens, Flora played with a silk scarf. She could be a rich and famous movie star or just let the silk scarf float on the air as she ran about. Then she looked and saw Beth playing. She asked her "would you like to try on my silk scarf". Without hesitation Beth said yes, (not knowing that this was the silk scarf of doom). Flora said "Beth let me know when the scarf is too tight on you neck". Flora began to tighten the scarf around Beth's neck until she could no longer breath or speak. Frannie turned just in time to see Beth in distress. "Stop, you're killing the baby" she yelled. She saved Beth from the scarf of doom.

On one end of the street they live on was a horse and buggy rental and at the other end of the street was the city dump and not far from their house was the river. Willa would tell her kids not to play in the city dump or the river, but the kids motto was what Willa don't know won't get us a spanking.

They would put on their mother's dresses to cover their clothing from the river mud and like a little procession make their way to the river. Certainly Willa would never see her four dresses covered with river mud and her four little girls, ages nine down to three mind you, wet and smelling like the river. Willa had to have been a genius because she always knew just where they had been. Spanking were generously given to each little swimmer. When the sun was hot and the chicken were boring, off to the river would go the little swimmers.

Beth favorite pastime was running, jumping, doing flips and climbing trees, so much so that she was nicknamed monkey by her family. One warm summer day Beth and her sisters decided to go cherry picking. Fruit grew wild in the patches of wooded areas near their home. Anyway, if they were able to gather a sufficient amount of cherries, maybe they could get their mom to make them a pie. They got sacks to carry their cherries and started off for the woods, monkey running and jumping along the way. It was always her job to climb up the tree and throw down the fruit, and this time was no different, up the tree Beth went. She could see birds enjoying the red ripe cherries. She ate some, put some in her sack, and threw some down to her sisters who were waiting under the tree. Beth noticed the birds that were once enjoying the cherries were now flying in crazy loops as if the were dizzy. She also felt dizzy and out of the tree she feel, tipsy from the wild cherries. After that day she would eat the cherries after she had come down from the tree.

Once Flora set Beth's hair aflame with an oil lamp. The story went like this, Beth had long braids that hug down her back. As she and her sisters ascended the staircase with oil lamps in their hands, Flora, who was walking behind Beth, took the end of one of Beth's braids and put it down into her lamp. Needless to say, Beth's braid went up in flames and Flora began to beat out the fire. The house was full of the smell of burnt hair. Willa knew just what happened and who did it when she saw Beth's hair and it was spanking time for Flora.

The family had moved to a house with indoor plumbing and electricity, no more ice box, no more oil lamps, no more fireplace, and no more outhouse.

The girls now were going into their teen years. They were going to dances and making goo goo eyes at young men. When it came to dancing, no one could out dance Adeline on the dance floor. Her jitterbug would cause a crowd every time. She and Frannie would go out with their friends but they wouldn't take Beth with them much because fifteen and sixteen year olds don't always want thirteen year old siblings around. Flora had started working in the steel mill where she eventually met Alfred Grant and they married.

Willa began to date Robson Ball and soon he became part of the family. Their first son was Robson Dent born in August of 1934. His nickname was Shorty because he was the shortest one in the house at the time. Then came along Edwin Dent in 1940, he was the color of light brown fudge so they nicknamed him Fudgie. In 1942 Geordie Dent was born, they nickname him Piggy.

Frannie began dating Wilson Davies, everyone called him "Tootee". Adeline had also started secretly seeing a man that was living at the same boarding house that her father Robson lived in. Thaddeus Herald was his name, he was twenty four years her senior, tall, and looked to be more Irish than African American. They ran off together and Robson Dent, her father, was furious that his teenage daughter had run off with this man. He went to Willa's house and demanded to know what she was going to do about Adeline running off. Willa replied "nothing, she know where I am when she want to come home". Robson stormed out of the house, but Adeline did come back right before Christmas. Adeline's son, Thaddeus Jameson Dent was also born in December 1944. Frannie and Tootee also had a son in December of 1944. Frannie named him Wilson Davies jr. They married not to long after Wilson jr. was born.

# CHAPTER 7

## Growing Up

There is not one perfect family tree. If there was perfection in man, we wouldn't need Salvation. The bible say that "we have all sinned and come short of the glory of God". We are just what we are made up of, from what we are taught by our traditions and environment to our very propensity to do something. Our family is far from being an exception to the rules because there is none. The elephant that weighs heavy on our family tree's branches is chemical addiction, a violent temper, and a foresight (some call it a veil ) that only could be balanced by God. When a baby is said to be born with a veil, it is born with a part of the placenta covering the face like a veil. It is traditionally said that one born with a veil is also born with the ability to see supernatural things.

It wasn't always easy for my mother Beth and her sibling growing up. Knife fights were commonplace in their household when their mother Willa and Robson had to much to drink. Grandma Willa was considered to be less quick tempered than her sister Sarah. Aunt Sarah sold alcohol from her house but they had to get out of her house with it. She also cooked and cleaned for a house of ill repute. Sarah had no toleration for disrespect. She would cut a person within an inch of their life if they disrespected her or her house. I remember being told a story about just that. The story went like this, when aunt Sarah was young she was slender, short, and very nice looking woman. Well, she was walking down the street, I imagine on her way home from work, when she past by a man swinging some keys on a chain. As she pasted by, he threw the keys out and hit her on the butt and said something about her being a pretty young gal. She turned and look at him and said "If you're here when I get back I'm going to kill you". He didn't take her at her word and stayed right there. When she returned she almost cut him to death. I can't say who stopped her that day, but I'm glad God changed her.

One night aunt Sarah went to a church meeting and got the Holy Ghost, and all the descendants of grandma Willa and aunt Sarah's household can take a minute to praise God for that day. God healed her from TB, Diabetes, and cancer just to name some. He did a complete work in her life. She also married Mitchell Brandy, who loved her with all his heart.

When the Lord call her to preach, her Papa wasn't happy with it and nether was her biological mother Cassie Winfield. Aunt Sarah looked her mother up after God had changed her life. Her mother had remarried and had three more daughters, Efia, Angie, and Doty Davies. Grandma Cassie, who's last name was now Davies, told aunt Sarah that she was a fool because she and all granny Cassie's children were born with a gift ( a veil) and that she could make money from that gift. In Cassie Winfield's mind giving readings was a way for Sarah and all her children to make a good living. I'm glad Sarah wanted to please God rather than man.

In October 1949 Zion Holiness Church held is first service in aunt Sarah's dining room. She never looked back, from her dining room to Perry street and from Perry street to Auburn street the church grow. God blessed her ministry greatly. People were healed of all manner of illnesses and substance abuse. Aunt Sarah and Uncle Mitch's family grow also. Delia, Uncle Mitch's daughter from his first marriage, came to live with them. Delia was expecting her son Geordie at the time. Aunt Sarah and Uncle Mitch had their first and only child together. Their daughter Emily was born about a year later in 1952. Aunt Sarah became the matriarch of her and grandma Willa's family after grandma Willa died when her heart gave out during a gallbladder operation in about 1955. All of grandma Willa's kids were on their own by then, all except Edwin, who was fifteen at the time, and Geordie, who was thirteen. Edwin went to live with his sister Frannie and her kids. Geordie went to live with Beth, my mother, before we were born. Aunt Frannie had seven children altogether, Wilson, Edmond, Mitchell, Ilene, Victoria, Harus and Steward. Aunt Adeline also had seven children, Jameson, Jadalyn, Dorothy, Dewey, Rebecca, Mona and Aldy.

Granny Cassie Davies came up north to visit my mother Beth and the rest of the family. She asked Beth "Do ya know where dat ooman Jennie lib what sold my husband Jack?". The funny thing is Papa Jack had pasted away by this time and Mama Jennie had remarried. Beth answered Granny

Cassie "you mean Mama Jennie?" Granny Cassie said "Yes, take me ta her house. I'm goin ta kick her tail!" Beth told her "I'm not going to take you to mama's house so you two old lady can fight. I'll take you shopping instead". They got ready for their shopping trip and walked to the bus stop. The bus arrived and they both got on. Beth said to granny "Here is a seat for you near the front of the bus". Granny, being from the south was not accustom to seating in the front of the bus. She said to Beth in a whisper "Oh no Beth, le's go ta da back, to many white folks in front". Beth told her that it would be ok to be seated in the front and that she wouldn't have to give up her seat later. The white folks were seated all over the bus up north. Granny sat down uneasily and took her bus ride to the store. Although they were not yet able to try on clothing in the store, times were beginning to change. Maybe the change was coming a little to fast for Granny.

One day Aunt Adeline came to my mother's house with a worried look on her face. It was clear she had been drinking as she came close to my mother's face to whisper. When someone in the family had done something mischievous it was a habit to speak of the act in a sheepish whisper. She said "I think I've killed Leon". Leon was the father of Aunt Adeline's daughter Rebecca. My mother asked "What happened?" also at a whisper. Aunt Adeline went on to tell her how her and Uncle Leon had been drinking and they began to argue. Uncle Leon hit her during the argument and proceeded to drink until he passed out. Aunt Adeline then tied Uncle Leon to the chair that he was seated on. She went to their old washer and removed the rubber seal that went around the inside of it. She began to beat him with the rubber seal until he could no longer respond to the beating. Fear then took hold to Aunt Adeline and she ran to Beth's house. In the mean time Uncle Leon came to, got himself free and went to the Police station and made a report about the beating. The Police arrested Aunt Adeline and grandpa Robson's cousin Glen went to bail her out. On the way home Aunt Adeline said to cousin Glen "can you believe they want to charge me with assault and battery?". Cousin Glen responded "Yes, and you did it. Ya salted him, battered um, and would da eat um if ya could".

Aunt Adeline lived with her husband Gordon, her son Dewey's father Shawn and Rebecca's father Leon all at the same time. One by one they became disenchanted and moved out. After that Aunt Adeline start seeing Jameson, Aldy and Mona's father. One Sunday morning after drinking all night Aunt Adeline and uncle Jameson were in the street fussing and fighting with one another when along come Pastor Spofford. Pastor Spofford, feeling dignified and self-righteous with himself, called out to the two "Ya should be ashamed of yourself fighting on a Sunday morning. You should be on your way to church with me". Aunt Adeline stopped fighting with uncle Jameson and called back to the Preacher "You should be ashamed of yourself because you're on your way to hell". Uncle Jameson took this time to make his escape and ran. Aunt Adeline, with her attention still on Pastor Spofford, began to name all the women the Preacher had affairs with. Aunt Adeline reiterated, "you got your nerve. You're going right to hell". The Preacher, feeling less dignified and self-righteous with himself, stepped quickly down the street hoping no one else had overheard the conversation between him and Aunt Adeline. Before Pastor Spofford could get out of church service that afternoon it was all over town what aunt Adeline had said to him that morning.

Aunt Flora and her husband live in West Mifflin and only had one daughter, Tisa. Tisa was born in 1958 the same year my oldest sister Victoria was born. Both of them were like long awaited Princesses and they got everything they could ever want or need. Tisa had a way of thinking, that if you can take something, why pay for it. Later I can recall her calling that way of doing things her five finger discount. I can remember their visits to our home when we lived in the housing projects. As a person entered our apartment by the front door, they would step into a large living room, dining room area, from that room ran a long hallway. To the left hand side as one walked down the hall was the kitchen, the bathroom next, and two bedroom. At the very end of the hall one faced a third bedroom with the backdoor to your right. Well, one day I was sitting on the floor playing dolls in the back bedroom on the right and Tisa walked in and sat on the floor next to me. Before she could tell me much about the new purse her mom had gotten her the backdoor opened and in walked Dorothy and Victoria, two of our older cousins. They came into the room where Tisa and I were sitting on the floor, with a look of mischief on their faces that would send shivers down any kids spine that ever had them for a babysitter. Close the door, Dorothy said to Victoria and she did. I could only think, what are they going to do to us now, normally they got paid for torture sessions and I didn't remember hearing my mom say she was going out. Victoria looks at Tisa with a look that would cause anyone to confess. "Where is my watch?" she said as relief came over me. Tisa with indignation in her voice said "I don't have your watch!". Hay, I believed her but thought it best not to get involved, so I stayed silent. Dorothy said search her, as she snatched Tisa's purse from her hand and poured it out on the floor. They began patting her down with the skill of a Police officer and out came the watch. They took the watch and out the door they went. I thought, normally when she would take something that was my sister's, my sister would tell aunt Flora and aunt Flora would ask Tisa if she had it. You know, Tisa would say she didn't take it and that would be that. My sister would have to search Tisa room the next time we visited her house to get her things back. Tisa was always so much shorter than my sister Vickie and soon we all grow taller than Tisa. It was always funny to me to hear her call us, everyone younger than Vickie that is, her little cousin. Her size never stopped her from standing up for herself, right or wrong. I don't know how she felt when our cousins Dorothy and Victoria search her or when my oldest sister Vickie and cousin Rebecca would search her room for their clothing and jewelry. Once they got their things no more would be said about it.

There was a candy store right down the road from the projects where we lived. I recall one nice warm summer day when my cousin Rebecca, my sister Vickie, my sister Maria, my sister Adeline and I was trying to think up a way to make money to buy candy. We didn't have any lemons to make lemonade to sale. So we sat there thinking and Vickie said "I know we can sale fortunes". She went on, "we could make a tent on the playground, write fortunes on paper and sale them for a penny". We made our tent and put a little table and chair inside the tent. Vickie sat behind the table and Rebecca sat next to her and the rest of us ran around the playground getting customers. Most kids only got one or two fortunes but one little girl wanted to have Vickie read her a fortune paper every five minutes. I thought what a waste of money, people will buy anything. Rebecca told Vickie that the little girl liked her youngest brother Aldy. So when the little girl came back for the third or forth time Vickie put her hand to her head as though she was thinking of something and said a dramatic "wait, I see something". The little girl replied "what" as if she believed her. Vickie slowly put out her other hand for the penny the little girl was holding. As the girl gave her the penny, Vickie said "Oh yes, its becoming more clearer". She went on "I see you getting married to, oh its getting dim, I think that its Aldy". The girl smiled a big smile. Vickie said "perhaps another penny will help me see more clearly". The girl said I will ask my mom for more money. She came back three or four more times before her mom made her stop coming. We had enough money for all of us to get candy that day.

One nice spring day I was walking to the store to get some candy when two teenage girl past me by. One turned and said aren't you one of those crazy Dents, as if that was our name. It never was just aren't you a Dent, it was always aren't you a crazy Dent. I told the girl yes, just wanting to go my way but the girl asked are you Hicks' sister? He's crazy, she said. Hicks is what everyone called aunt Adeline's son Dewey. I said no he is my cousin.

Then you are Harus and Steward's sister? I said no they are my cousins, my aunt Frannie's kids. The one girl looked at the other and said with a slight laugh, they are all crazy. The other girl said I thought they were all sisters and brothers. I walked away thinking nineteen kids would be a lot of kids for one household.

Once, just before the start of school, my mother, aunt Frannie, and aunt Adeline took us to get new shoes. I would say they had about ten kids altogether in tow. My mother had her five kids, Alexis in a stroller, aunt Frannie had Harus and Steward, and aunt Adeline had Rebecca, Mona and Aldy. Anyway, we got to Pick Away Shoes Store and all the kids were excited to get new shoes. A man took our shoe sizes and help us all find just the right pair of shoes. Everyone thought their shoes was the best looking pair ever. As we got to the checkout, every kid wanted their shoes paid for first. Each kid had to place the shoes on the checkout desk according to what parent was paying at the time. Each kid rang out "these are my shoes" as the checkout lady tried to remember who's shoes belonged to whom. Mona, who I don't think understood the order of the checkout, continued to try to hand the lady her shoes. Telling the lady "these are my shoes lady, don't forget my shoes, these are my shoes". Mona's mouth ran the whole time we were at the checkout. The lady's face turned red and she began to look flustered and confused, but finally every kid had the shoes bagged and in hand. As we walked out the store and down the street, aunt Adeline stopped in her tracks as if a moment of clarity had hit her. She cried out in a frustrated voice, "Oh Mona, you made me forget to pay for your shoes!". We all went back to the store. I think I may have seen terror in the checkout lady's eyes as we reentered the store, but she was nice about it all.

My sister Adeline and I would spend a lot of time together growing up. We were like night and day, I was painfully shy and she was very outgoing. I always felt like I was just a tagalong although I was the older of the two of us. Her and her friends, at about nine or ten years old, went through a smoking stage. You would think they would have stolen cigarettes from their homes to smoke, but no, Helen, the littlest one in the group, came outside with cherry cigars. They smoked the cigars until they felt sick, then they throw them away and were off to think up something else to do.

My sister Maria, growing up, was into school and band until she start liking boys. She even ran for Home Coming Queen in high school once.

As a kid, I thought Maria was the smartest and bravest kid ever. There was a bully, wecalled Big Foot, that use to beat-up on me and Adeline a lot. One day we were playing with in our living room with our cousin Aldy. The living room door was open and the bully passed by. He happened to see a toy broom on our living room floor and told us to give it to him or else. Adeline and I told him no, because we knew he was afraid to come inside the apartment to get it. He told Aldy that he would beat him up when he came outside if he didn't give him the broom. Aldy gave him the broom, and shortly after the bully left Maria came in the house. We told her what had happen and she said three of you let one bully take a toy from you, I'm going to get that toy back. Maria got that toy back with no problem. I wasn't afraid of that bully anymore.

Years before my mother Beth and her second husband Poncho McGowan were ever married, they went to visit cousin Frannie Sue and her husband Rene. Aunt Adeline and uncle Jameson ( Aldy and Mona's dad) was there also with Mrs. Joy Ann, another friend. As one would come up to cousin Frannie Sue's house, you would see a long porch with two doors. One door led into the living room and the other door led into the kitchen. As the evening of laughing, talking and drinking went on, Rene got up and went into the kitchen and out the kitchen door. Before anyone could think twice, Rene came running in the front door and leaped onto Mrs. Joy Ann that was setting on the couch at the time. As he was fighting with her and fussing at her for being in his house, cousin Frannie Sue got him in a headlock and began choking the air out of him all the time trying to explain to him that he is why the could never have people over. As Rene went limp, uncle Jameson pried cousin Frannie Sue grip from his neck. Rene pulls himself together and went into the kitchen and out the door. Again, he runs through the door and leaps on the woman and again cousin Frannie Sue chokes him to within an inch of his life and uncle Jameson saves him from her grip. Out the kitchen door and in the front door Rene runs again, but when he got free from cousin Frannie Sue's grip this time, he went into the kitchen and made a call to the police. He told the police to come and get him because he was drunk and trashing his own house. The police came and took him to jail and cousin Frannie Sue had to bail him out the next day.

There was a teen dance hall on second street called Bertha's. It was owned by Rusty, a police officer and his wife Bertha. Most of the teens that lived around the area would go to Bertha's to meet and dance. They didn't really have gangs at that time in the area were we lived, but they did have drug dealers. Some teens would sale drugs like it was a summer job at fast food restaurant. My sister Vickie started hanging out at Bertha's when she was about twelve years old. She always liked being around kids much to old for her. Getting high and fighting was also top on her list of things she liked to do as a teenager. The funny thing is the people Vickie called her good old friends were the ones she was fighting with all the time. Bertha's was where they would go to work out their differences. I never could keep it straight when they were friends or fighting.

Once some one asked Mr. Rusty why he had even opened Bertha's dance hall. He answered that he wanted a safe place for his kids to hang out.

Bertha's dance hall closed after Mr. Rusty died, when I was about thirteen or fourteen. Although I didn't hang out at Bertha's, I was sad when Mr. Rusty died. It seemed as if second street died the day Mr. Rusty did.

Mr. Rusty's brother Vincent, a light skin man with light brown eyes, was my sister Alexis's father. I don't remember much about Mr. Vincent because he moved to New York not to long after Alexis was born.

Alexis could whistle before she could walk or talk and when she could walk, running, jumping, and summersaults, was what she did all day long.

I can remember when Alexis was about two or three at the most and a mouse went running across the living room floor. We all screamed and jumped for the nearest chair or couch. Alexis, who was holding a story book in her hand at the time, screamed unconvincingly and threw the book with precision accuracy at the mouse. Needless to say, she killed the mouse and became the hero of the day. Alexis was always short for her age, in preschool the teacher would always refer to her as the baby. She did have a friend growing up that was shorter than her. I think his name was Keith, he talked a lot and knew all the gossip. Keith talked very fast and excited as he would tell Alexis the latest news he had overheard. I would pretend not to hear them as I tried not to laugh at the intensity on his little face.

I started to date Roland Atkins, a boy from school, when I was about twelve or thirteen. Roland was the youngest of eleven sisters and brothers. He grew up in the projects near the elementary school with his mom and siblings. Rowe was a tall, thin, light skin young man with a large afro. Adeline started to dating Donny Bradford around that same time as I started dating Rowe. Donny's family was so big that people would call them the house of many. Don was also tall and light skin with light brown eyes, a large afro and a heavy voice. My other two sister also were now dating, except Alexis, she started much later than us. When Alexis started dating, Keith seem to just go his way like most of our friends did when we began to date. Some boys stuck round a short time and was gone, but Rowe who dated me and Donny who dated Adeline, became like a part of the family.

One day when Rowe was visiting me, my cousin Aldy and Martin, Aunt Frannie's oldest grandson, came into the house as they would do often. Most of the time they would be laughing at nothing until my mother would put them out. This time they were not kicked out right away. They said to me and Rowe "we almost starved to death". They went on to say "we were looking all over the kitchen for food in Aldy's house and then we found some cold bologna in the refrigerator and it saved our lives". They began to sing "cold bologna, I could da been dead. Cold bologna, Mayonnaise and bread". Later we found that the songs and laughing the two eleven year olds were doing was weed inspired.

There is one family reunion that will always stick in the back of my mind. When I was about fourteen years old my mother told us that cousin Frannie Sue, her uncle Saul Dent's daughter, was putting together a family reunion. They were going to have it at one of the parks in Ohio. It sounded like it would be a fun trip, after all, Ohio had some pretty good amusement parks like Sea World, Geauga Lake, or Cedar Point. I asked my mother if it would be alright to bring my boyfriend Rowe along if he paid his own way, so she checked with cousin Frannie Sue and said it would be ok.

The day of the trip came and two buses pulled up in the projects. Everyone was excited to be going to the park. Cousin Frannie Sue began calling names from a list of paper she had in her hand and we began boarding the buses. Rowe and I sat together and my mom and sister's also boarded the same bus as we did. As we settled in our seats, Aunt Adeline and Buddy Pal, who was one of the town drunks, entered the bus already sauced up. Rowe, who found everything humorous, asked my if Buddy Pal was part of my family. I could feel my face get warm as I hoped it was just a passing question and that when we got to the park he would be amused by the fun we would have there and not by my family. I told him that Buddy Pal was just invited by Aunt Adeline because they were friends. Then cousin Nola Pearl got on the bus with her friend Buffalo Bear who was also an alcoholic. Buffalo Bear exclaimed to all on the bus, "I'm family, I'm a Dent too". My hopes of an uneventful trip was fading fast.

As we arrived at City Park in Ohio, Buddy Pal looked out the bus window and said in a loud voice "this isn't Geauga Lake, unless we have to get out and jog around a lake". All the kids laughed who was on the bus. As we got off the bus, I saw so many kids that looked like us. Some with sandy brown hair and dark skin. They were family alright and before long my cousin Hicks, who was also full of sauce, had the kids from Pennsylvania playing football and fighting with the kids from Ohio and getting a big kick out of it.

Buddy Pal soon passed out at the picnic table so some of the young men put him on the bus to sleep it off. Buddy Pal was a nice man more or less, he was just an alcoholic. Sometimes he would shoot up his house and furniture thinking that he saw people setting on his couch. It seemed like he had to buy a new couch every couple of months. Buddy Pal slept on the bus for the rest of the trip.

As the family reunion came to a close, we all began boarding the two buses again. Some kids boarded the bus before me and ran to the back of the bus pass Buddy Pal, who was sleeping on one of the seats near the back. The kids yelled "oow, he peed on his self!". Buddy Pal was wet all down the front of his paints and sleeping like a baby. Aunt Adeline entered the bus passing by cousin Pauline, who was one of her running buddies. Cousin Pauline and aunt Adeline liked to go out drinking together and when they were drunk they would start a fight with each other just to keep the night interesting. When aunt Adeline passed cousin Pauline, she said "I don't know why Sharon came, she ain't no Dent". Cousin Pauline had adopted two of her sister's children, Sharon and her brother, and they were very much part of the Dent family. Anyway, cousin Nola Pearl was setting to the right of aunt Adeline as she passed by giving her remark. Cousin Nola Pearl said "Sharon has just as much right to be here as anyone else". Aunt Adeline, who was now standing next to cousin Frannie Sue, one seat behind cousin Nola Pearl, reached over cousin Frannie Sue to grab hold of cousin Nola Pearl. As cousin Nola Pearl and aunt Adeline struggled with one another, they fall on top of cousin Frannie Sue causing her wig to fall off. Family members separated the two ladies and they took their seats. As I thought to myself, I should had got on the other bus, cousin Pauline's voice rang out "I know that had to be one of uncle Rob's kids". As if grandpa Robson's branch of the family tree was any worse than any other branch. Aunt Adeline cried out "I'm going to show you what uncle Rob's kids can do when we get off this bus".

The bus driver let cousin Pauline and Sharon off the bus near their home and proceeded on to the projects were we live. As we exited our bus a ruckus came from the second bus and people were hauling Hicks off the bus fussing up a storm. Hicks had been fighting someone on the bus and threw a beer bottle through the bus window. That was the last family reunion I went to.

My grandfather, Daddy Bob came to live with us after my grandmother and father passed away. He seem to really take to my boyfriend Rowe. No one could do anything better that him. If anyone was on there way to the store, they would ask Daddy Bob if he wanted them to pick up anything for him. He would always say "No, Rowe will be here soon". He always wanted the same thing from the store every time; prunes, pound cake or devil's-food cake. Although, one time he told Rowe not to get him pound cake anymore because it made his mouth water to much. I thought, isn't that why you eat sweets. He sometimes had a funny way of putting things.

One day Rowe came to visit and Daddy Bob came to him with an empty pill bottle. He told Rowe that he was out of his medicine and that he really needed his medicine. So we went as fast as we could to the pharmacy. We told the pharmacist that my grandfather needed his prescription right away. The pharmacist took the pill bottle and looked at it. Then he walk over to the aspirin on a nearby shelf, opened a bottle and poured them into Daddy Bob's prescription bottle. Rowe and I look at the pharmacist with a stunned look on our faces. I asked "That's all that was in that bottle?". The pharmacist smiled and said "next time he needs this prescription just pour a bottle of aspirin into the bottle. It's just aspirin". Daddy Bob was happy to get his medicine and we never told him it was just aspirin.

Daddy Bob loved the ball game, baseball and football. It seemed like a ball game was coming on the TV or radio all the time. I recall many times, our family intensely gazing at the television screen with the hero of the story just about to find out who the secret killer was. Out of the corner of our eyes Daddy Bob would move slowly closer to the TV and the hero would move slowly closer to the room that the killer is in. Just as the hero reaches for the door, Daddy Bob changes the TV channel. Daddy Bob would announce "Ball game coming on baby". The room would erupt with "Aw man! The ball game come on after this show". We never would get to find out who the secret killer was.

Rowe and I would walk all over Duquesne, the town we grew up in. We would see Vickie and her friends it seemed like everywhere. Rowe would always say "man, your sister is always running around like Peter Pan, when you lest expected it she would pop up saying hi Rowe!". Vickie and some of the other teens would ask Rowe for a joint. Although he didn't smoke them, they were easy to come by. Other kids would just give them to him and he would open them up and mix them with Parsley, Chive, leaves or anything he could find. He would give them to anyone who would ask him for a joint. I remember Vickie asking him for a joint and he gave her one mixed with acorn leaves. The next time we saw her she said it was the best joint she ever had. He said to me they stay so high all the time they don't know what they are smoking. She was growing up to be a hand full for our mother. I guess we all were from time to time.

Maria had her first son, Raymond when she was about sixteen. Raymond was like the little Prince of the house. He could talk before he could walk. I could hear him now "get my roller, get my roller" he would say in a desperate voice as Rowe and I would start out the door. We took him everywhere with us. Adeline hand Donny jr. a year after Raymond, when she was about fifteen. Little Donny and Raymond became close as peanut butter and jelly.

We all started going to church again not to long after little Donny was born. We had to take two buses to the Hill district were Aunt Sarah's church was located. We were always rushing around trying to get out the door on time. Daddy Bob's most famous line was "if ya start on time, you'll be on time". Out the door we would rush to make it to the bus stop on time.

A lady in church, we called sister Dallas, prided herself in being a prophet. When church service was lively she would close her eyes, walk around and begin to "prophesy". Every time it was the same "somebody is going to die, die, die! Somebody is going to die". My godmother, Thelma Wilmington, would wallow behind her with a distressed look on her face asking "Who is going to die? Who is going to die?". Aunt Sarah would say under her breath to Evangelist Smart, who was seating next to her in the pulpit, "We are all going to die one day". Aunt Sarah would say "God always has an if. If you don't stop, I will or if you do this, I will". There is always a way of escape for them that obey God. Thelma Wilmington had a very bad heart and was very mischievous to say the less. She was a cougar as it is called. She was in her late sixties or early seventies and secretly dating men that were in their twenties. Thelma Wilmington was said to be aunt Sarah's cousin. Her mother said papa Jack, Sarah's father was her bother who ran away from the family as a teenager.

It was a long cold ride in the winter to church but surprisingly Rowe and Don went to church with us. We all hated the long ride and Vickie, who was always the first to protest, told my mother she wanted to go to a closer church. My mother said "well, you're eighteen now, go and tell Aunt Sarah you quit because you want to go to a closer church". As we made our way to the bus stop Vickie continued to fuss "I will tell them I quit.

She don't think I will but that church is just too far away". We made it to church service and as it began to come to a end the Pastor asked if anyone wanted prayer or had something to say. Vickie stepped forward and before she could get the words, I quit, out of her mouth, the Holy Ghost fall on her and she began to speak with tongues. Before anyone could think about it my sister Adeline also began to speak with tongues. My sister Maria and I were ushering that day, but I and then Maria began speaking with tongues. No one quit church that day. Don, Rowe and Rowe's best friend Drew were baptized not long after that and Rowe also received the Holy Ghost.

Drew had moved to Pennsylvania from Alabama to live with his uncle Willis and aunt Joan. Drew accent was very thick and Rowe seemed to be the only one that could understand him at times. Rowe became like a interpreter for Drew and stood by him when people would laugh at the way Drew talked. Drew was a good friend to Rowe, like a brother.

# CHAPTER 8

## Branching out

Rowe began working in the steel mill after he graduated high school. Maria, who graduated the same year as Rowe, also began working for US Steel and eventually got a duplexes for our mother and her to live in. Vickie had graduated the year before Rowe and Maria, and was now working for Duquesne Light. Vickie and Rowe also began preaching every now and then at aunt Sarah's church.

Rowe and I got married when I was seventeen and he was eighteen. Drew was Rowe's best man and Donny was a usher. I graduated high school the same year we were married. People told Rowe that it would never last because we were to young but its been over thirty years now. There has been ups and downs but I wouldn't want to spend my life with any other. We got our first house when I was eighteen. It was just down the street from where Maria and our mother were living.

Donny and my sister Adeline married a year after Roland and I. Adeline was expecting her and Don's second child. Don also began working in the steel mill. He and my sister lived with my mom after they were married. Don was a lady's man and loved staying out late with his friends doing only God knows what. He also worked as a strong arm for one of his family members that was a loan shark. Adeline would tell him often that if he didn't change his ways someone would find him died one day. When Adeline became angry with Don she would eat the lunch that she had packed for him before he could take in to work with him the next day. Don died in a car accident before their daughter Natasha could be born. Adeline never seemed to be the same after Don died. She seemed to be more downhearted although she did eventually remarried and have two more kids.

Rowe and I were expecting our first baby six years after we were married. A time that should have been full of joy and happiness was instead bitter sweet. US Steel closed a lot of the plants in the area and many people including Rowe and Maria were out of a job. It was a time of stress and sorrow for the people in Pittsburgh Pennsylvania. Some people even killed themselves because they could no longer take care of their families. Rowe could only find a part time job to help pay to continue our medical benefits that we had when he was working in the mill. We also had to get welfare benefits to help ends meet. I was in and out of the hospital a lot due to complications with my pregnancy. Our son Josiah was born a month premature in October of 1984. He was four pounds and six ounces with some of the fingers missing on both of his hands. Josiah was never Handicap in his own eyes or ours. He learned to hold his bottle and to feed himself just like any other baby.

On Josiah's second Christmas my mother had give us a small Christmas tree that sat on top of a table. I put the tree inside Josiah's playpen because he was now walking and I didn't want him to pull the tree over.

I gave Josiah his bottle and started to make lunch. Josiah came back into the kitchen before long wanting his bottle. I asked him where was the bottle I gave him. He took me over to the playpen were the Christmas tree seat. Around the Christmas tree among the neatly rapped gifts were my shoes, Rowe's shoes, some of Josiah's old toys and his bottle. He was too little to reach the tree so he was throwing things at it. That Christmas season if we couldn't find something, more than likely Josiah had thrown it under the Christmas tree.

The government promised all the misplaced workers TRA money to help them to go to school and to get back on their feet. When Rowe would go to the unemployment office to sign up for his unemployment check the line would be long enough to reach out the building and around the corner. The line for TRA money was just as long as the line to sign up for unemployment.

After standing in the unemployment line half the day, Rowe got into the line for TRA money. Hours seem to pass and then finally he made it to the desk. The lady behind the desk looked at him and say "The government has not put any money in the TRA benefits so you may as well go home". The next time he went back to sign up for his unemployment check that line still run out the building but the TRA line was shorter. So after signing up for his check, he got into the TRA line again. When Rowe got to the desk the lady said "You were here before. Didn't I tell you there was no

TRA money?". Rowe left but the next time he came to sign up for his unemployment check there was no line at the TRA desk. He went up to the TRA desk and when the lady saw him she pretended to be busy. Rowe stayed right there until she finally came over to the desk. The lady looked at him and said "I will give you an application for TRA just to keep you from coming back to my desk again". Not even a week later they said on the evening news that the government had funds for the TRA program and that only those that already had an application in could get the funds. Rowe completed four years of college in about three years with the help of God and the TRA program. Rowe got a job in Wichita Kansas and before we moved the TRA program also gave him the back benefits that they should have given him when he was unemployed. He was also able to bless the church by paying off a thousand dollar pledge he had made just before he got laid off and he paid for three choir robes for the church. We used the rest of the money to move to Kansas. After we moved to Kansas Rowe, completed getting his Masters Degree.

Living in Kansas seemed so different to me. People would say hello to me even if they didn't know me. Sometimes I would look all around to see who they were talking to and find that they were talking to me. Rowe had come out to Kansas before Josiah and me. He was living in a motel near his job and had just gotten our apartment right before he came to get us. Rowe's coworkers told him that he would need to get an air conditioner here in Kansas. In Pennsylvania we didn't need an air conditioner. A fan was sufficient enough to keep the house cool. The first week we were in Kansas Rowe had to go to Kansas City for training. It was so hot in our apartment that week that Josiah and I had to stand in the shower with our swimming suits on for most of the day. When Rowe came home from Kansas City he got an air conditioner from the store that same day.

The summer before Josiah started kindergarten Rowe sign him up for a Taekwondo class. Josiah had not, as of that time, learn to tie his shoes. Every time I would try to teach him he would be a little strong headed and tell me "I gat it, I gat it. I know how to draw my name". In all marshal arts classes the student have to take off their shoes. At the end of the class Master Kim look and saw Josiah hand me his shoe. Kim said to me "He no tie his shoes?". I said "no". He looked at Josiah and said "You big boy. You put shoes on and tie them". Josiah cried as he struggled to put his shoes on and tried to tie them. He didn't get them tied but he did get them on. I took note in my mind that day that he never told Master Kim "I know how to drew my name". After class each time Josiah would make a mad dash for the door with his shoes in his hands. He would say to me in a worried voice "Let's go mom, let's go". If Kim saw Josiah trying to run out the door with his shoes in his hands he would stop him, make Josiah put his shoes on and try to tie them. Some of the mothers wanted to know why I wasn't upset with Kim. I just told them that I wasn't. Sometimes little boys need the guides of the strong males in there life and not to be babied all the time. Like my husband Rowe, Kim didn't see a baby or a helpless little boy when he looked at Josiah. He saw a boy that would some day have to become a man. Josiah did learn to tie his shoes that summer and to my surprise he wanted to take more Taekwondo classes with Master Kim. Josiah also began to take swimming classes that same year.

There was nine and a half years between Josiah and our second son Elijah. Elijah was born in March of 1994. About a week after Eli was born, I had heart failure. I had a dry cough for sometime but didn't think much about it. That evening as I was giving the baby his bath, it became harder and harder for me to breath. I thought maybe I had bronchitis or something. Rowe call my Dr. and he had Rowe to take me to the hospital right away. They were putting oxygen up my nose, taking blood from my arm and putting monitors on my chest. I looked over at Rowe holding our new born in his arms and little Josiah at his side. He looked so worried, so I told him to take the kids home and that I would be alright. The Dr. told Rowe that I may have to get a new heart but by the mercy of God I didn't have to.

My mother came out to Kansas to help Rowe with the kids until I got out of the hospital. We had been in Kansas about five years by that time and when my mom walked into the hospital room to see me I was happy. The first thing she said to me was "Boy, how fat you've gotten". I smiled and tried not to show that I was hurt by her comment. Rowe and the kids had also come to the hospital with her. Rowe handed me the baby to hold. The nurse, who was also in the room, told me not to hold the baby close to the heart monitors on my chest. The baby began to fuss so I handed him back to Rowe and they soon went home.

Not many days later I was able to go home myself. I felt useless but I was determined to get healthy. I was weak and not able to do much of anything. I knew I would have to build up my strength again. If I just took a walk to the end of my street and back, I would need a nap. Rowe had become like mom and dad for the kids. After my mother went back to Pennsylvania, I started taking short walks around the apartment complex. I began to grow a little stronger everyday.

One day after a walk I sat on the steps in front of my apartment. Two Mexican ladies with a little baby walked up to me. I said hello and asked what the baby's name was. They didn't speak English, but I had been trying to learn how to speak Spanish from a cassette. I tried the question in Spanish and to my shock they understood me. They said his name was Andy and asked our names. I was understanding most of their words until all the greetings were over. I did understand that Marie was Andy's mother and Olivia was Marie's mother. Olivia had come from Mexico to help her daughter Marie with her new baby.

Olivia came to visit me everyday after that day we met and she would help me with my baby. She almost seemed like an angle sent from God. She made sweaters for the baby as she sat and talked to me even if I didn't understand it all. She even gave me knitting lessons, although I never really made anything.

When the baby was six month old Rowe's job moved us to Garden City Kansas. I told Olivia that we were moving so she gave my her address in Mexico and I gave her my new address. I was going to miss Olivia, she was a blessing to my family.

The town we moved to was small with feed lots and meat packing plants all around. The air was awful, as the little boy that lived next door to us would say "It smelled like a elephant pooped outside". It was bitter cold in the winter and hot as a oven in the summer. Not many African Americans lived in Garden City.

The kids were growing quickly. Rowe enrolled Elijah into a preschool class one summer. It seemed like every time I came to pick Elijah up I could hear his teacher franticly yelling his name or something like it. "Ellis! Elisha!" I would hear. I looked though the little window in the door. I could see Elijah running as fast as he could around the room laughing with the teacher close behind him. "Ellis!" she yelled as she finally got hold of the giggling kid.

With her face red as a beet, his teacher brought her hand up in the air, hesitating just a moment she brought it down lightly on his butt. I told Rowe how Elijah was behaving in school. He didn't believe me so I told him to pick Elijah up from school the next time he had class. Rowe said Elijah had all the kids running and giggling that day. I know the teacher was happy to see that class end. It took a little growing up but Elijah is a honor student in school now.

With Elijah the terrible twos lasted from age one and a half until five years old. When Rowe and I would take him and Josiah to church we would sit with them between us on the pew. The very second we took our eyes off him, under the pews in front of us and into the pulpit or running around the church he would go. We would just take the kids home when it got to be too much for that day. He and Josiah were like night and day. Josiah would always sit nicely at church.

Lisa Martinez, a sister from church and I started giving in home bible studies to the new converts and shut-in with the Pastor's ok. Elijah began to sit more quietly at the bible studies and at church. Maybe he thought he was our helper. He would help us pray for the people at the end of the studies even when we really didn't need his help. I think he just needed something to do. We would do just three bible studies a week; one study in English with Ann a new covert who was going through a divorce and had just recovered from a brain aneurism. The second bible study of the day was in Spanish with Juanita and her many kids. Lisa would teach the Spanish bible study. Our last bible study of the day was with an old lady named Wilma and her toothless pomeranian dog named Bear. I think the ladies mostly enjoyed having someone to talk to each week.

One Sunday there was a guest speaker at the church we were attending. After preaching, the minister came up to Rowe and told him that the Lord had called him to start a church. Rowe knew that he had a call on his life even when we lived back in Pennsylvania but no one here in Kansas knew about it but God. He just kept the man's words in his heart. It would still be some time before he would become a Pastor.

Lisa and her husband Fernando had been attending that church for about a year before my family and I came along. Although Fernando had attended a Pentecostal church in the past, Lisa had not. They both seemed determined to live a dedicated life for God.

Lisa Martinez and I became good friends. Lisa told me that she had been a alcoholic before God changed her life. I knew that most of the time alcoholism or drug addiction was normally a mask for underlying problems. Many time when we would pray together before we would go to teach bible study or at church, she would say she was angry or she was hurting or call for her mother. If I would ask her way, she would say she didn't remember or that she didn't know. So I asked God to help me understand why my friend was like that. He told me that they were broken fragments of her wounded past. She had been molested as a child by a friend of her family. Some wounds are so painful that some people are only able to let go of them a little bit at a time. The bible talks about some that were healed as they went. As she was healed, she was able to tell other that they could be healed also.

One day Lisa and her husband Fernando came to visit. They said they were having home bible studies and would like to start a church. Rowe and I said that we would help them all we could. I went to their next bible study and the home was overflowing with people. They needed a bigger place for the people. Lisa and I looked all over town for a building to have service in. We found a big commercial garage cheap. The church grow overwhelmingly fast. Fernando and Lisa began to feel the stress of the ministry on their home life. They felt it would be best to get a new Pastor over the church.

Fernando and his family call a Spanish Pentecostal organization and asked them to send them a Pastor for the church. The church had been bilingual but when the new Pastor came he changed it to just Spanish speaking.

Rowe's job moved the family again. We were going back to Wichita, Kansas but Lisa and I stayed in touch.

Rowe and I began Bethel Apostolic Church. The first person that came through the door was an elderly Mexican man that spoke very little English. I used my bilingual bible to help change the Sunday school lessons to Spanish and to help me translate the preaching. He was a migrant worker and only would be there for a season. The person that came into the church next was a lady that couldn't hear and her two kids. I went to the store and got a book on signing and a note book. We were soon able to talk to each other. Her name was Juanita and she had been divorced. She told me that she was a preacher's daughter. For some reason she thought she would turn into a man when she die. I told her that we will be changed into an incorruptible body. I also told her that the bible say that we would be like the angles and they don't marry nor are they given in marriage. I was surprised that most of what she knew of the bible she learned from her brother when they were little children. She didn't learn to sign until she was an adult.

Juanita and her kids attended Bethel Apostolic church a couple of years until people from her old church start visiting them. They went back to that church because it was much bigger than Bethel. Soon they stopped going to church anywhere. Juanita start living a lesbian life style and her ex-husband took the kids from her.

One day Juanita came over to the church as Rowe and I were gathering things to take to a church meeting in the park. She began weeping and crying. She told me that she was thinking about how here children would sing in church and would want to study the bible but now they hated church and never wanted to go again. Their father had told them about their mother being molested by their grandfather, who was a Pentecostal Pastor. She had never told the kids about it. I told her that she could stay if she'd like, but as most people that looked at our little store front church, she just wanted prayer and then she went on her way.

I got a call on the phone one morning. It was Ann from Garden City. She was in the one of the hospital here in Wichita with another aneurism. She asked me if I could come right away. When I got to the hospital her family had not arrived yet from Garden City and they were about to take her into surgery. Her Dr. told me that she had a ten percent chance of making it through the surgery but if she didn't have it she would die. I prayed with Ann and then they took her into surgery. Her family arrived, I told them what the Dr. said and that she was in surgery. I knew she would be in surgery for hours so I told her family that I was going home and would be back later. I went home, told Rowe what was going on and asked him to be praying for Ann. We had dinner and I went back to the hospital. Ann was out of surgery but she had not come to yet. Her family told me they had to go because it was a long ride back to Garden. Ann came to after they left. She looked at me with a sad face and said "my family didn't come". I told her that they did come and that they had stayed until she had come out of surgery.

When Ann was about to go home from the hospital I told her to take things slow. I knew even though she felt ok she still needed time to heal. She told me that she was going to church that night. Although Ann didn't speak Spanish, she had been attending the church that Lisa and her husband started. I said to her "You know its four hours from here to Garden City". She only said I'll be ok. That night I got a call from Ann. In a frantic voice, she said "I died in church tonight". Knowing that I wasn't talking to a ghost on the phone, I said "How do you know you died". She began to tell my how she went to church and before she could seat down on a pew she died. She went on to say that the people at church prayed her back to life and the Pastor told her to go home and not come back. I told her that when people die their muscles relax and they go to the bathroom on themselves. She said "I did!" I'm not much for telling people I told you so. I just told her take it slow.

Ann died about two years later of another aneurism. As she got sicker, she stopped going to church. She didn't want anyone to see her that way.

Her daughters called me after her death, they said they couldn't find my phone number before hand. Rowe and I helped to pay for Ann's funeral.

One night a young Mexican couple came to church service. Only the man could speak a little English and his wife only spoke Spanish. He said that he was trying to start a church and that he had been a member of the same church organization as the church we helped in Garden City, Kansas. He asked us if we could fellowship with them and help them when we could. We did and another church was born.

Being a Pastor can be highly stressful on ones family. The church the young Mexican couple began started growing but their marriage didn't make it. That church changed Pastors four times. Each Pastors family shattering under the emotional pressure. Two of the Pastors' marriages end in divorce and one of the Pastors was deported from the country. Finally that church got a Pastor that could stand under the pressure of the job.

We made many friends in helping the Pastors and Ministers of the Spanish Pentecostal organization, but Bethel Apostolic Church became a refuge for us in times of stress.

My sister Vickie started a church in Pittsburgh Pennsylvania around the time that Bethel Apostolic began. She named the church Zion Holiness church after the church aunt Sarah started. Like Bethel, Zion was very small and people would come for prayer and healings then go to a bigger church. Although Vickie was far from Kansas, we became encouragement for each other. I think it takes all kinds of ministries, big and small, to reach all kinds of people.

Years later, as I was preparing to go to a church revival in Pennsylvania, I was talking on the phone with one of the Evangelist from Brazil that would be helping to run the revival. He asked me if my family ever had family reunions. I guess he had delusions about preaching to my family and getting them all saved. That would have been nice but knowing my family and with the last family reunion I went to in mind, I quickly told him I don't go to family reunions. I could just imagine the fun my family would have with him once they had a little to much to drink. I told him he would only be meeting the family members that would come to church service. I know he didn't have any idea what he was asking, poor thing. He only knew Pastor Vickie Brandon (my sister Vickie), her husband John and some of my family members after God changed their life. He would also get to meet Maria and Alexis and their families. They both were married with six kids in each family.

I believe that all family trees have wild breaches. The Bible calls us wild olive breaches that the Lord grafts into believing Israel. So we look back at what we were and know that we can look up because the Lord knows what we can be in him or what we will be without him.

# ACKNOWLEDGMENTS

I would like to thank my husband and my family for their help, love and support. It's not always easy to make a step in a new direction but one would never know what they could accomplish if they give up before they try.

With the help of family stories, the internet and my own memory, I tried to be as accurate as I could. I found that one story can be as vast as the many people telling it, so like the saying "this is my story and I'm sticking to it."

I also would like to acknowledge the help of DNA testing that traced our family roots back to the Bakole and Biaka tribes of Africa.

www.ingramcontent.com/pod-product-compliance
Lightning Source LLC
Chambersburg PA
CBHW031333290526
45784CB00014B/2623